I0816870

ntatives of the UNITED STATES

ngress assembled.

n events it becomes necessary for one people to
e connected them with another, and to
~~[illegible]~~ as
rth the separate and equal ~~[illegible]~~ station to
re's god entitle them, a decent respect
res that they should declare the causes
separation.

self-evident; ~~[illegible]~~, that all men ar
they are endowed by their creator with eq
at ~~from that equal creation they derive~~
rights; that
e, among ~~which~~ these are ~~[illegible]~~
appiness; that to secure these rights ~~ends~~, go
g men, deriving their just powers from
t whenever any form of government
ends, it is the right of the people to alter
w government, laying it's foundation on

ALSO BY WALTER ISAACSON

Elon Musk

The Code Breaker: Jennifer Doudna, Gene Editing, and the Future of the Human Race

Leonardo da Vinci

The Innovators: How a Group of Hackers, Geniuses, and Geeks Created the Digital Revolution

Steve Jobs

American Sketches

Einstein: His Life and Universe

Benjamin Franklin: An American Life

Kissinger: A Biography

The Wise Men: Six Friends and the World They Made (with Evan Thomas)

Pro and Con

Franklin, Adams, and Jefferson drafting the
Declaration of Independence at Jefferson's lodgings on
Market Street in Philadelphia, painted by Jean Leon Gerome Ferris.

The Greatest Sentence Ever Written

Walter Isaacson

Simon & Schuster

New York Amsterdam/Antwerp London Toronto Sydney/Melbourne New Delhi

For Leonard Lauder

Simon & Schuster
1230 Avenue of the Americas
New York, NY 10020

First Simon & Schuster hardcover edition November 2025

SIMON & SCHUSTER and colophon are registered trademarks of Simon & Schuster, LLC

Interior design by Ruth Lee-Mui

Manufactured in the United States of America

7 9 10 8 6

Library of Congress Control Number has been applied for.

ISBN 978-1-9821-8131-4
ISBN 978-1-9821-8133-8 (ebook)

IMAGE CREDITS: Endpaper: The Library of Congress; iv: Photo 12 / Alamy

Contents

The Greatest Sentence Ever Written

1776

"We hold these truths to be sacred . . ."

Sacred? No. That doesn't sound right.

But that's how Thomas Jefferson wrote it in his first draft.

Benjamin Franklin, who was on the five-person drafting committee with Jefferson, crossed out "sacred," using the heavy backslash marks he had often used as a printer, and wrote in "self-evident." The declaration they were writing was intended to herald a new type of nation, one in which our rights are based on reason, not the dictates or dogma of religion.

But then the sentence invokes the "Creator." In Jefferson's first draft, he wrote that men are created equal and "from that equal creation they derive rights." That phrase is crossed out, this time with a different pen, and replaced with "endowed by their Creator" with rights. Given Jefferson's skeptical views on religion, it does not seem like a phrase he would use. It was probably suggested by John Adams, whose religious views were more conventional.

Thus we see, in the editing of the second sentence of the Declaration of Independence, our Founders balancing the role of divine providence and that of reason in determining our rights.

It became the greatest sentence ever crafted by human hand.

We hold these truths to be self-evident,
that all men are created equal,
that they are endowed by their Creator with certain unalienable Rights,
that among these are Life, Liberty and the pursuit of Happiness.

On its 250th birthday, each of its words and concepts bears scrutiny and appreciation.

We

Let's start at the beginning: the word *We*.

The first word of the sentence is also the first word in our Constitution, drafted eleven years later, which begins, "We the people . . ."

That phrase, *We the people*, is as profound as it is simple. Our governance is based not on the divine right of kings or the power imposed by emperors and conquerors. It is based on a compact, a social contract, that we the people have entered into.

Let's hold off, for the moment, addressing the question that women, Blacks, Native Americans, and others might ask: "What do you mean *we*?" We'll deal with that when we get to the discussion of "all men." For now, let's focus on the idea that the authority of any government, since the dawn of civilization, should be based on the concept of a social contract.

Social contract theory gained currency during the Enlightenment, beginning in the seventeenth century. The English philosopher Thomas Hobbes, in his 1651 book, *Leviathan*, hypothesized that humans in primitive times lived in "a state of nature," with no government. Lacking rules, this "anarchic war of all against all" meant that life for most people was "solitary, poor, nasty, brutish and short." In order to emerge from this state of nature, people eventually came together and agreed to submit themselves to governing authorities.

The Founders, and in particular Jefferson, were mainly influenced by a version of the social contract theory that was developed by John Locke in his 1689 *Second Treatise of Government*. "The only way whereby any one divests himself of his natural liberty, and puts on the bonds of civil society, is by agreeing with other men to join and unite into a community for their comfortable, safe, and peaceable living one amongst another, in a secure enjoyment of their properties," he wrote.

The Scottish philosopher David Hume refined the concept in his 1748 essay, "Of the Original Contract," by explaining how governments derive their authority. "The people, if we trace government to its first origin in the woods, are the source of all power and jurisdiction, and voluntarily, for the sake of peace and order, abandoned their native liberty and received laws," he wrote. Jean-Jacques Rousseau, whose 1762 book, *The Social Contract*, Jefferson had in his library, defined the *we* as the general will of the people: "Each of us puts his person and all his power in common under the supreme direction of the general will."

Jefferson was invoking this collective will, not just the will of the sixty men gathered in Philadelphia, when he began his sentence, "We hold these truths . . ."

Self-Evident Truths

What did Franklin mean when he deleted "sacred and undeniable" in Jefferson's draft and put in the phrase "self-evident"?

That phrase has a very specific meaning in analytic philosophy, more than just a fancy way to say "obvious." The concept was developed by Franklin's close friend Hume.

In 1759, when Franklin was in Britain to lobby for the rights of the colonies, he visited Scotland and got to know Hume, the greatest English-language philosopher of his era. They began a regular correspondence on matters ranging from how new words get invented to the best way to construct a lightning rod, and Franklin regularly sent him wry tales about human foibles that he had written for his *Poor Richard's Almanack* or for the amusement of friends.

In hopes of enlisting Hume to the side of the colonies in their disputes with Britain, Franklin visited him in

Edinburgh in late 1771 and ended up staying for more than a month. Hume had just built a new house, and he boasted that the sheep's head soup made by his cook was the best in Europe. "David Hume, agreeable to the precepts of the gospel, has received the stranger and I now live with him," Franklin reported to a friend. They spent their evenings together discussing ideas of natural rights, social contracts, and the revolutionary stirrings rising in the American colonies.

Hume developed a theory, later known as "Hume's fork," that there are two types of truths. One type is "synthetic" truths, which are statements whose truth is contingent on empirical evidence and observations. For example, "London is bigger than Philadelphia." The other type is "analytic" truths, ones that are true by reason and definition. For example, "All bachelors are unmarried." To confirm a synthetic truth, you have to observe real-world facts, such as calculating how many people live in London compared to Philadelphia. But that is not the case with analytic truths. To know that all bachelors are unmarried, you do not have to go around surveying bachelors to see if any of them have wives. "Propositions of this kind are discoverable by the mere operation of thought," Hume wrote. Their truth is *self-evident*.

By labeling as self-evident the truths in their sentence, Franklin and the drafting committee implied that they were true by definition, "discoverable by the mere operation of thought," not contingent on observations. For example, the statement that men are created equal did not arise from observing different people and determining whether they were indeed equal; it instead derived from the fact that they all are autonomous individuals who were "created equally free and independent," as explained in the Virginia Declaration of Rights, written by George Mason a month before the Declaration of Independence.

But let's be honest. Labeling their assertions of "these truths" as "self-evident" was not entirely correct. They were, in fact, quite controversial, even revolutionary.

All Men

All men. A phrase that seems on the surface to be very inclusive was, in fact, very restrictive, and its eventual expansion, in fits and starts, is a key element in the narrative of America.

Did the Founders mean the word *men* to refer to all humankind?

The words *man* and *men* have often been used, historically and to some extent today, to refer to humankind in general. "Man is a social animal," Aristotle said. The Greek word he used, *ánthrōpos*, can be translated as *man* but refers to all humans. Locke writes of "the dignity of man." The French Assembly, when it launched its own revolution in 1789, titled its manifesto "The Rights of Man." In Old English, the word *wer* was used for a male and *wīf* was used for a female, while the word *mann* generally meant any person, male or female, young or old.

Is this what the Founders meant when they used the phrase "all men"? Did they mean it to refer to all people?

Actually, no. Even if the rhetorical flourish of "all men" conveyed a broad scope, they consciously and intentionally did not mean in most instances to include women, slaves, Native Americans, and in some cases even non–property owners.

Free women were accorded some rights at the time, but not the rights to vote, hold office, or have full property ownership. The major thinkers of the Enlightenment, most notably Rousseau, argued that women's roles were domestic and subordinate to the roles of men.

The Continental Congress never debated the issue of women's political rights. Abigail Adams famously urged her husband, John, in 1776 to "remember the ladies" and not give men "unlimited power" over women. But John wrote back, "I cannot but laugh . . . We know better than to repeal our Masculine systems."

Created Equal

When the drafters declared that "all men are created equal," they made it clear that they intended this assertion to be a "self-evident" truth, based on reason, not a truth based on observation. People differ widely in their talents and abilities. But the drafters' point was that all men were autonomous individuals in the state of nature and came together to create the social contract. As a result, they all were equal in terms of the political and social rights that arose from that contract.

Specifically, the Founders were rejecting the idea, fundamental in the British system, that there were certain hereditary social classes, beginning with the royalty and aristocracy, that had more rights than other classes.

But in making this argument, they had to wrestle with the fact that there was one hereditary class of people in the American colonies who were considered property, not equal creations. In 1776, there were about 500,000 enslaved people in the colonies, which was one-fifth of the population.

The Virginia Declaration of Rights, adopted just as Jefferson and his committee were beginning work in June 1776, tried to finesse the glaring contradiction. Its author, George Mason, originally wrote, "All Men are created equally free and independent and have certain inherent natural Rights." That was amended to add the clause "when they enter into a state of society." The amendment was proposed explicitly to exclude slaves.

Jefferson didn't use this dodge. He simply wrote, "All men are created equal and independant," and then, making it even punchier, he deleted "and independant."

Jefferson's original draft called the slave trade "a cruel war against human nature" and resoundingly condemned King George III for imposing it on the colonies. In his "Notes on the State of Virginia" in 1785, he called slavery a "moral depravity" and "hideous blot."

Nevertheless, exhibiting the moral contradiction at the core of America's founding, Jefferson himself enslaved more than six hundred men, women, and children. These included Sally Hemings, who became his mistress, and the children they had together, who remained enslaved. He freed only a few of his slaves during his life, and even in his will did not free most of them, not even Hemings, though he kept his promise to her by freeing their children.

Jefferson's philosophical mentor Locke also fell prey to these contradictions. The only form of enslavement Locke justifies in his *Second Treatise* is of captives taken in a just war, not humans sold into slavery. Nevertheless, he profited from the slave trade as a shareholder in the Royal African Company and helped draft the Constitutions of Carolina, which declared that "every freeman of Carolina shall have absolute power and authority over his negro slaves."

John Adams expressed his disapproval of slavery when he was on the committee with Jefferson drafting the Declaration. "I always feel a kind of indignation at the sight of a slave," he wrote a friend in 1776, "and I am persuaded that the practice of holding men in slavery is equally repugnant to the spirit of liberty and the ideas of happiness." Nevertheless, he did not favor immediate abolition. "The subject is too dangerous to be touched in public," he wrote another friend. And when he later became president, he limited U.S. involvement in the slave trade but did not try to abolish slavery itself.

His wife, Abigail, was more outspoken, saying that the Southern slaveholding delegates' "pretensions to liberty are a mockery" when they hold "hundreds in chains." She even addressed Jefferson directly. "The practice of slavery is a reproach to any people who boast of liberty and equality," she wrote to him in 1804. "How can those who advocate the rights of man hold their fellow creatures in chains? It is a contradiction that must wound the conscience of every honest man."

As for Franklin, his moral trajectory mirrored that of American history. Throughout his life, he kept a ledger of the mistakes he had made and how he had tried to rectify them. The greatest, he realized, was that as a printer in Philadelphia he owned two slaves who worked in his shop. By the 1760s, they had wandered off, and Franklin made no effort to prevent that. He joined an organization that established schools for Blacks in America. His wife, Deborah, enrolled her house servants in the Philadelphia school, and after visiting it Franklin wrote of his "higher opinions of the natural capacities of the Black race."

He became increasingly outspoken against slavery in the 1770s. In an essay for the *London Chronicle*, he decried, using language stronger than almost any other Founder, the "constant butchery of the human species by this pestilent detestable traffic in the bodies and souls of men." He wrote in a similar vein to the Philadelphia physician Benjamin Rush. "I hope in time that the friends to liberty and humanity will get the better of a practice that has so long disgraced our nation and religion."

Franklin's journey culminated in 1787, when he accepted, at age eighty-one, the presidency of the Pennsylvania Society for Promoting the Abolition of Slavery. On behalf of the Society, Franklin presented a petition to Congress. "Mankind are all formed by the same Almighty Being, alike objects of his care, and equally designed for the enjoyment of happiness," it declared. The duty of Congress was to secure "the blessings of liberty to the People of the United States," and this should be done "without distinction of color."

Franklin's petition was denounced by the defenders of slavery, most notably Congressman James Jackson of Georgia, who declared that the Bible had sanctioned slavery and that, without it, there would be no one to do the hard and hot work on plantations. It was the perfect setup for Franklin's last great essay, written less than a month before he died. He wrote it as a parody in the form of a purported speech given by an official in Algiers. The parody speech attacked a petition asking for an end to the practice of capturing and enslaving white European Christians to work in Algeria. "If we forbear to make slaves of their people, who in this hot climate are to cultivate our lands?" the speech asked rhetorically, and then it proceeded to mirror the arguments Congressman Jackson had made in favor of enslaving Africans.

Jefferson's passages in his draft of the Declaration

denouncing the slave trade as "a cruel war against human nature" were edited out by the delegates before it was approved. Of the fifty-six signers, forty-one owned slaves. All thirteen of the colonies permitted slavery. Shortly after the Declaration was signed, the English abolitionist Thomas Day wrote, "If there be an object truly ridiculous in nature, it is an American patriot, signing resolutions of independency with the one hand, and with the other brandishing a whip over his affrighted slaves."

But the moral arc of American history, during the subsequent 250 years, mirrors the personal narrative of Franklin's life. Abraham Lincoln opened his Gettysburg Address in 1863 by referring directly to the second sentence of the Declaration: "Four score and seven years ago, our fathers brought forth on this continent a new nation, conceived in Liberty, and dedicated to the proposition that all men are created equal." At a cost of close to 620,000 lives, including 7,058 buried in the cemetery he dedicated that day in Gettysburg, the Civil War brought an end to slavery. "The arc of the moral universe is long, but it bends toward justice," Martin Luther King Jr. said, echoing an 1853 sermon by the abolitionist minister Theodore Parker. But it's important to remember that the arc did not bend itself. It was, and remains, a constant American struggle to make the phrase "all men are created equal" truly inclusive.

Endowed by Their Creator

Jefferson built on his assertion that men are "created equal" by arguing, in his first draft, "that from that equal creation they derive rights." Once again, the committee tweaked his language. "They are endowed by their Creator" with rights, the final version declares. The phrase was more felicitous and memorable but did not mean exactly the same thing. It asserted that a creator had endowed them their rights, rather than that those rights were derived from their equal creation in the state of nature.

Jefferson's original formulation reflected his religious outlook, known as Deism. Like Franklin and the many other Deists among the Founders, he believed in a supreme being or creator but rejected the idea of a personalized God who acts through supernatural interventions, divine revelations, and miracles, and he denied the divinity of Jesus. Deists derive their understanding of God from reason and observation of the natural world, making them adherents of "the laws of nature and of nature's god," as Jefferson put it, echoing Voltaire, in the first sentence of the Declaration. Deists believe that God set the universe in motion with wondrous laws but did not intervene in human affairs after that. Deism was the creed of most thinkers of the Enlightenment, the eighteenth-century Age of Reason that emphasized rationality, science, individualism, and natural rights. Its leaders included Locke, Hume, Voltaire, Rousseau, and, in America, Franklin and Jefferson.

Jefferson's Deism led him to create what became known as the Jefferson Bible; he used a razor and glue to create a version that focused solely on Jesus's moral teachings and cut out all mentions of Jesus's miracles, resurrection, and divinity. In a 1787 letter to his nephew Peter Carr, Jefferson advised, "Question with boldness even the existence of a God; because, if there be one, he must more approve of the homage of reason."

Adams's religious views, although influenced by Deism, were a little more traditional than Jefferson's. In a letter to Jefferson in 1817, he wrote, "The existence of a God is so obvious that no man in his senses can doubt it." Nevertheless, as a Unitarian, he expressed doubts about traditional Christian theology and in another letter to Jefferson criticized the doctrine of "the divinity of Christ." His focus, he told Jefferson, was on God as a creator, the "great Architect of the Universe," and on "the wisdom and benevolence of his government of the universe." Because of his more traditional focus on God's role as a benevolent creator, he was most likely the committee member who suggested that the phrase "endowed by their creator" replace Jefferson's "from that equal creation they derive rights."

As for Franklin, the final summation of his religious thinking came the month before he died, in response to questions from the Rev. Ezra Stiles, president of Yale. Franklin began by restating his basic creed, "I believe in one God, Creator of the Universe," adding that "the most acceptable service we render to him is doing good to his other children." Then he addressed Stiles's question about whether he believed in the divinity of Jesus, providing a surprisingly candid and wry response. "I have," he declared, "some doubts as to his divinity, though it is a question I do not dogmatize upon, having never studied it, and think it needless to busy myself with it now, when I expect soon an opportunity of knowing the truth with less trouble."

Certain Unalienable Rights

The final version of the Declaration of Independence declares that people are endowed "with certain unalienable Rights." That's not exactly how Jefferson wrote it. He used the word *inalienable*, which is how the phrase is inscribed on the Jefferson Memorial. But Adams, when he made a copy of Jefferson's rough draft, changed it to *unalienable*. That is the way it appeared in the parchment approved on July 4.

The words were used interchangeably at the time, and there is no clear distinction in meaning. Perhaps it was just a transcription error, or maybe Adams or some aspiring copy editor in Congress had a personal preference. I'm with Jefferson. I like *inalienable*. It's more felicitous.

OK, but what does it mean? For that, it's again useful to go back to what George Mason had published a month earlier in his Virginia Declaration of Rights: "All men are by nature equally free and independent and have certain inherent rights, of which, when they enter into a state of society, they cannot, by any compact, deprive or divest their posterity." In other words, there are certain rights that are *inherent* to a person's existence in a state of nature that, even when they make a social contract, they cannot divest. Nor can any government or monarch deprive them of these rights.

Life, Liberty and the Pursuit of Happiness

In Locke's original development of his contract theory, he identifies three fundamental rights: life, liberty, and property. When men enter into a social contract to empower a government, he writes, it is done "with an intention in every one the better to preserve himself, his liberty and property."

Property is a cornerstone of Locke's theory of justice. By owning the fruits of their labor, people preserve their liberty and individual rights. A person in the state of nature joins into a social contract, Locke wrote, to "preserve his property, that is, his life, liberty and estate, against the injuries and attempts of other men."

In Virginia's Declaration of Rights, Mason turned Locke's philosophy into a precursor of Jefferson's sentence:

"All men are by nature equally free and independent and have certain inherent rights . . . namely, the enjoyment of life and liberty, with the means of acquiring and possessing property, and pursuing and obtaining happiness and safety."

In Jefferson's formulation, "the pursuit of happiness" is just a simpler way to say all of that. It is your right—and your opportunity—to seek fulfillment, meaning, and well-being however you personally see fit.

Common Ground

These truths became the creed that bound a diverse group of pilgrims and immigrants into one nation. For a people with many different beliefs and backgrounds, it defined our common ground and aspirations.

As we reach the 250th anniversary of the Declaration, we are embroiled in increasingly polarized debates over policies ranging from healthcare and housing to immigration and the role of religion in our society. One way to restore stability to our politics is to look at issues through the two ideals that are at the heart of the Declaration's key sentence: common ground and the pursuit of the American Dream.

The concept *common ground* has always been part of humanity's struggle to create a good society. Its simplest manifestation was a physical space: the land that was designated as "the commons." In feudal England, that was the land where the commoners—yes, that's where the word *commoners* comes from—could all graze their herds. When the first English settlers came to America, this space was set aside in their towns, such as the Boston Commons and the Cambridge Commons.

Even the concept of private property, and the pursuit of property, grew out of the existence of common ground. Locke in his *Second Treatise* declared that humans can create private property by combining their labor with things they take from nature. But he included a famous limitation, known as the Lockean Proviso: only "where there is enough, and as good, left in common for others."

The idea of the commons was not just about land. Societies have always put certain basic goods into the commons, such as schools, libraries, police, and fire protection. These are called the *communiter bona*, the goods in common.

In colonial Boston, the Puritan minister Cotton Mather wrote a book titled *Essays to Do Good*, in which he said that people could best serve God by creating institutions that benefited the common good. Franklin, deeply influenced by Mather's book, set up in Philadelphia a "Leather-apron Club" of tradesmen and small business owners, which launched a street-sweeping corps, volunteer fire and night watchman corps, hospital, library, and Academy for the Education of Youth, which became the University of Pennsylvania.

The library served as a commons where both poor tradesmen and wealthy merchants would come to read books. The spread of such libraries, Franklin later wrote, "made our common tradesmen and farmers as intelligent as most gentlemen from other countries."

Creating this type of common ground, where people were treated with equal dignity, was the best way, he said, to serve their creator. As he put it in the motto he wrote for the library, *Communiter Bona profundere Deum est*, To pour forth benefits for the common good is divine. But it also served a more practical purpose. It nourished the conditions for democracy in a free-market system.

Alexis de Tocqueville, who wins the award for being the least read but most quoted author about America, made an assertion that I think is wrong. He argued that there was an inherent struggle in America between two opposing impulses: the spirit of rugged individualism versus the conflicting spirit of creating associations and common grounds. But, in fact, the two strands are woven together, the warp and woof of the American fabric. Fiercely independent individuals were equally fiercely devoted to their community and its commons, and they voluntarily came together in barn raisings and knitting bees and militias and social aid societies to serve the common good.

• • •

Juxtaposed against the commons is the right, important for a healthy economy, to also have property that is private. In Locke's time, Parliament passed a series of laws that were known as the Enclosure Acts. They allowed certain people to build fences to enclose some of the common land for their private use. These enclosures led to more efficient production, even an agricultural revolution that greatly increased the nation's wealth.

Both freedom and economic growth require that we allow individuals to reap the benefits that come from their labor. Our system does, and should, give ample rewards to builders and entrepreneurs and those who work hard, take risks, and even just have good luck.

But in doing so, we should keep in mind the moral and practical value of the commons. Back in feudal times, the existence of common grounds, those things to which everyone had the same rights, helped stabilize a society with disparities of wealth by giving people a stake in the social order.

The same principle holds today in a free-market system that allows the accumulation of great wealth. By making sure there remains, as Locke said, enough in the commons, we not only show our moral compassion to others less fortunate, we also nurture the social bonds that temper resentments, political polarization, and populist backlash.

Most of our political debates these days are over which goods—Healthcare? Housing? Schools? More police?—should be provided for, at least to some extent, in the commons. It requires a balance.

Franklin and Jefferson understood balance. They were part of an Enlightenment era that embraced the scientific method of testing and revising beliefs based on evidence. Both of them studied Isaac Newton, whose mechanics explained how contending forces could be brought into equilibrium. Their goal on contentious issues was not to triumph but to find the right balance, an art that has been lost today. Compromisers may not make great heroes, Franklin liked to say, but they do make great democracies.

The American Dream

The commons serves another purpose. It enables opportunity. That is the moral purpose of the commons. It forms the foundation for creating a land of opportunity and what became known as "the American Dream."

That phrase was popularized by James Truslow Adams in his 1931 book, *The Epic of America*. "The American Dream," he wrote, "is not a dream of motor cars and high wages merely, but a dream of social order in which each man and each woman shall be able to attain to the fullest stature of which they are innately capable, and be recognized by others for what they are, regardless of the fortuitous circumstances of birth or position."

The example Adams used would have pleased Franklin: a library. He described the grandeur of the Library of Congress, open to all, and declared, "As one looks down on the general reading room, which alone contains ten thousand volumes which may be read without even the asking, one sees the seats filled with silent readers, old and young, rich and poor, black and white, the executive and the laborer, the general and the private, the noted scholar and the schoolboy, all reading at their own library provided by their own democracy. It has always seemed to me to be a perfect concrete example of the American dream."

In America these days, we have a lot of goods and services that we put in the commons, including libraries and national defense, police and fire departments, road-building and street-sweeping corps, schools, and even some access to healthcare. But there has also been a process of enclosure that has been eroding our common ground. The philosopher Michael Sandel calls this the "skyboxification" of America, whereby places and practices that used to be in commons are now roped off. We all used to sit in the stands at the ballpark and go through the same entrances, buying the same beer and soggy hot dogs. But now there are VIP entrances and skyboxes. We have separate lines at airports. We have more neighborhoods that are gated. And local public schools are often no longer the commons for kids of different economic backgrounds.

The same has happened with media and information and ideas. We go to our different culs-de-sac online, dive down different rabbit holes on the internet, listen to different ends of the talk radio dial, and let algorithms turn our social media feeds into echo chambers. The technology that promised to connect us found a better business model in dividing us.

This shrinkage of our commons led to the erosion of the American Dream's core principle, which is that we should be a land of opportunity for all. If you played by the rules, there would be good jobs at good wages, decent schools, safe streets, and—most important—the prospect of an even better life for your children.

For the past forty years, we pursued economic policies based on a consensus belief in free trade, free markets, free movement of capital, and free movement of people. This led to offshoring jobs, closing factories, and having immigrants to do low-paying work. These policies were, for the most part, intended to fuel economic growth, and in that regard they succeeded. They led to a fast-growing globalized economy that produced more overall wealth and consumer goods.

These policies also led to the rise of a meritocratic elite in America based on educational credentials. The economy and its rewards were geared to those who went to college; the 62 percent who never finished college ended up feeling resentful, or were made to feel it was their own fault that they were left behind.

Jefferson would have understood the trend toward a meritocratic elite. He favored creating what he called a "natural aristocracy" to replace the hereditary aristocracy that existed in England. In his *Notes on the State of Virginia*, he advocated a school system in which "the best geniuses [would be] selected, and continued six years, and the residue dismissed. By this means twenty of the best geniuses will be raked from the rubbish annually and be instructed at the public expense."

The approach of raking an elite from the rubbish and dismissing the residue did not turn out well. The entrenchment of a meritocratic elite came at the expense of community and the American Dream. The globalized economic system increased wealth, especially for the elite, but it reduced opportunities for those who used to have secure working-class jobs.

It created an economy where people could buy a flat-screen television very cheaply at Walmart on a Sunday night. But on Monday morning, they were no longer able to take the bus to a job at a local factory. Their grandparents, on a single income, could have a house, a car, and two or three kids. But they can't afford even a house.

Most problematic, it led to an economy where people could no longer believe that their kids would be better off than they were. It used to be easy for Americans to climb the economic ladder. Eighty percent of kids born in 1950 would go on to earn more, in inflation-adjusted dollars, than their parents had. But for kids born in the 1980s, there was less than a fifty percent chance of achieving the same financial success as their parents. *Less than fifty percent.* No wonder there was resentment and populist backlash.

Franklin correctly saw the danger of creating a meritocratic aristocracy. His proposals for what became the University of Pennsylvania were designed not to filter a new elite but to provide opportunities and enrichment for all young people to succeed as best they could, whatever their level of talent. He aimed at what he called "true merit," which he defined as "an inclination joined with an ability to serve mankind, one's country, friends and family, which . . . should indeed be the great aim and end of all learning."

Given the resentments and polarization that afflict us today, Franklin's wisdom should lead us to ask a basic question: What is the purpose of an economy? To increase wealth? Yes, that's good. Growth? Yes, also good. But the purpose of an economy is also something deeper. Its purpose is also to create a good society. A good, stable society where individuals can be free and flourish and live together in harmony. That requires nurturing the sense that we share common rights, common grounds, common truths, and common aspirations. Democracy depends on this.

Going Forward

At the official signing of the parchment copy of the Declaration, John Hancock, the president of the Continental Congress, wrote his name with his famous flourish. "There must be no pulling different ways," he insisted. "We must all hang together." Franklin replied, alluding to what would happen to them if their revolution failed, "Yes, we must, indeed, all hang together, or most assuredly we shall all hang separately."

As Franklin pointed out, our life-or-death challenge as a nation, whether it be in 1776 or 2026, is this: When there are so many forces dedicated to dividing us, how can we best hang together?

One way is by reflecting on our fundamental principles, the ones proclaimed in the Declaration's great sentence. Take any issue: healthcare, housing, schools, zoning, or whatever else is being debated around the dinner table or at

City Hall or in Congress. What policies and attitudes can we adopt, what balances can we strike, that will strengthen our common ground and the American Dream?

In an era without universal military service, what institutions can instill a sense of shared patriotic service across class lines? What policies can help give every kid an equal opportunity? And when it comes to our media and our daily discourse, how can we create news outlets, social media platforms, civil discussions, personal conversations, algorithms, and chatbots that seek to connect us to our common ground rather than inflaming our resentments, engaging us through enraging us, and harvesting clicks through sensationalism?

In short, we can try to be more like Franklin. He not only helped craft the sentence that defines our common ground. He lived it. He organized police, fire, and street-sweeping corps; a public library, hospital, and school; a widows' pension fund and a mutual insurance cooperative. He ran a newspaper that was dedicated to publishing a wide variety of opinions and following no party line. He bequeathed a revolving loan fund for young people to start enterprises. He donated to the building funds of each and every church in Philadelphia, and he helped lead the fundraising for a new hall that would provide a pulpit to visiting preachers of any belief, "so that even if the Mufti of Constantinople were to send a missionary to preach Mohammedanism to us, he would find a pulpit at his service." And on his deathbed, he was the largest individual donor to the Congregation Mikveh Israel, the first synagogue in Philadelphia. So when he died, 20,000 mourners watched his funeral procession, which was led by all the clergymen of every faith, including the local rabbi, walking arm-in-arm.

That's the ideal of common ground and the American Dream that our founders fought for 250 years ago. And that's what we must continue to fight for today so that we can preserve, for ourselves and our posterity, the rights and aspirations that we all share, including to life, liberty and the pursuit of happiness.

Appendices

The Drafting Process

Until 1776, most colonial leaders believed that America's disputes with Britain, mainly over taxation, were with Parliament's misguided ministers, not with the king himself nor the concept of being ruled by a monarch. To declare independence they had to take the daunting leap of abandoning this distinction. One thing that helped them do so was the publication, in January 1776, of an anonymous forty-seven-page pamphlet titled *Common Sense.*

Its author was a young Quaker from London named Thomas Paine, who had failed as a corset maker, been fired as a tax clerk, and then gained an introduction to Benjamin Franklin, who took a liking to him. Franklin helped him emigrate to Philadelphia, where he worked for a printer and honed his skills as an essayist. When Paine showed him the manuscript of *Common Sense*, Franklin offered his wholehearted support.

In prose that drew its power from being unadorned, Paine argued that hereditary rule was a historic abomination: "Of more worth is one honest man to society and in the sight of God, than all the crowned ruffians that ever lived." Thus, there was only one path for Americans: "Every thing that is right or natural pleads for separation."

Within weeks of its appearance in Philadelphia, the pamphlet sold an astonishing 120,000 copies. It galvanized the forces in the Continental Congress, which had gathered in Philadelphia, favoring outright revolution. On June 7, Virginia's Richard Henry Lee proposed a motion declaring, "These United Colonies are, and of right ought to be, free and independent states." As the Congress prepared to vote on that question, it appointed a committee to draft a declaration to explain the decision. It included Franklin, of course, and Thomas Jefferson and John Adams, as well as Connecticut merchant Roger Sherman and New York lawyer Robert Livingston.

Jefferson, at thirty-three, got the honor of drafting the document, which he did on a portable mahogany writing desk that he had designed and brought with him from Virginia. His writing style is graced with rolling cadences and mellifluous phrases, powerful despite their polish.

When he finished his first draft, Jefferson sent it to Franklin on the morning of Friday, June 21. "Will Doctor Franklin be so good as to peruse it," he wrote in his cover note, "and suggest such alterations as his more enlarged view of the subject will dictate?" (This original rough draft, appended below, is at the Library of Congress, and the final document is a few blocks away, at the National Archives.) For the next ten days, the committee made edits and tweaks, including those described above to his soaring second sentence.

On July 2, the Continental Congress took the momentous step of voting for independence and then considered the Declaration that had been written by Jefferson and his committee. They edited it heavily. Large sections were eviscerated, most notably the one that criticized the king for perpetuating the slave trade.

Jefferson was distraught. "I was sitting by Dr. Franklin," he recalled, "who perceived that I was not insensible to these mutilations." Franklin sought to console Jefferson by recounting a tale from when he was a young printer and a friend starting out in the hat-making business wanted a sign for his shop:

> *He composed it in these words, "John Thompson, hatter, makes and sells hats for ready money," with a figure of a hat subjoined.*

> *But he thought he would submit it to his friends for their amendments. The first he showed it to thought the word "Hatter" tautologous, because followed by the words "makes hats," which showed he was a hatter. It was struck out. The next observed that the word "makes" might as well be omitted, because his customers would not care who made the hats . . . He struck it out. A third said he thought the words "for ready money" were useless, as it was not the custom of the place to sell on credit. Everyone who purchased expected to pay. They were parted with; and the inscription now stood, "John Thompson sells hats." "Sells hats!" says his next friend; "why, nobody will expect you to give them away. What then is the use of that word?" It was stricken out, and "hats" followed, the rather as there was one painted on the board. So his inscription was reduced ultimately to "John Thompson," with the figure of a hat subjoined.*

The drafting committee had one last assignment: to print and distribute the Declaration to the colonies and, with a "decent respect to the opinions of mankind," the rest of the world. Philadelphia printer John Dunlap, a twenty-nine-year-old Irish immigrant, was chosen to make the first two hundred broadside copies, which he did working through the night of July 4. Franklin had long since retired as a printer, but he oversaw the process and chose the typeface: a font designed in 1722 by the London punch-cutter

William Caslon, which Franklin had imported and championed as a young printer. (This book is set in Caslon font.)

The next morning copies were sent to all of the colonial assemblies, militias, and top officers of the new Continental Army. General George Washington was defending New York City at the time. On July 9, when a copy of the Declaration reached him, he ordered his troops to assemble at 6:00 p.m. on the New York Commons in lower Manhattan. There he designated some of his officers to read the document aloud. Afterward, some of the crowd rushed to the four-thousand-pound equestrian statue of King George III a few blocks away, pulled it down, and cut off its head.

From John Locke's *Second Treatise of Government*, 1690

The state of nature has a law of nature to govern it, which obliges every one: and reason, which is that law, teaches all mankind, who will but consult it, that being all equal and independent, no one ought to harm another in his life, health, liberty, or possessions: for men being all the workmanship of one omnipotent, and infinitely wise maker; all the servants of one sovereign master, sent into the world by his order, and about his business; they are his property, whose workmanship they are, made to last during his, not one another's pleasure: and being furnished with like faculties, sharing all in one community of nature, there cannot be supposed any such subordination among us.

Every man has a property in his own person: this no body has any right to but himself. The labor of his body, and the work of his hands, we may say, are properly his . . . This labor being the unquestionable property of the laborer, no man but he can have a right to what that is once joined to, at least where there is enough, and as good, left in common for others.

The only way whereby any one divests himself of his natural liberty, and puts on the bonds of civil society, is by agreeing with other men to join and unite into a community for their comfortable, safe, and peaceable living one amongst another, in a secure enjoyment of their properties . . . When any number of men have so consented to make one community or government, they are thereby presently incorporated, and make one body politic, wherein the majority have a right to act.

If man in the state of nature be so free, as has been said; if he be absolute lord of his own person and possessions, equal to the greatest, and subject to no body, why will he part with his freedom? Why will he give up this empire, and subject himself to the dominion and control of any other power? To which it is obvious to answer, that . . . the enjoyment of the property he has in this state is very unsafe, very unsecure. This makes him willing to quit a condition, which, however free, is full of fears and continual dangers: and it is not without reason, that he seeks out, and is willing to join in society with others, who are already united, or have a mind to unite, for the mutual preservation of their lives, liberties and estates, which I call by the general name, property.

From Rousseau's *The Social Contract*, 1762

Man is born free, and everywhere he is in chains . . .

Since no man has a natural authority over his fellow, and force creates no right, we are left with agreements as the basis for all legitimate authority among men.

Let us take it that men have reached the point at which the obstacles to their survival in the state of nature overpower each individual's resources for maintaining himself in that state. So this primitive condition can't go on; the human race will perish unless it changes its manner of existence.

[Therefore people must] find a form of association that will bring the whole common force to bear on defending and protecting each associate's person and goods, doing this in such a way that each of them, while uniting himself with all, still obeys only himself and remains as free as before. There is the basic problem that is solved by the social contract.

Filtering out the inessentials, the social compact comes down to this: Each of us puts his person and all his power in common under the supreme direction of the general will, and, in our corporate capacity, we receive each member as an indivisible part of the whole.

From the Virginia Declaration of Rights, June 1776

That all men are by nature equally free and independent, and have certain inherent rights, of which, when they enter into a state of society, they cannot, by any compact, deprive or divest their posterity; namely, the enjoyment of life and liberty, with the means of acquiring and possessing property, and pursuing and obtaining happiness and safety.

That all power is vested in, and consequently derived from, the people; that magistrates are their trustees and servants, and at all times amenable to them . . .

That no free government, or the blessings of liberty, can be preserved to any people but by a firm adherence to justice, moderation, temperance, frugality, and virtue and by frequent recurrence to fundamental principles.

Jefferson's "Original Rough Draught" of the Declaration of Independence, June 1776

When in the course of human events it becomes necessary for a people to advance from that subordination in which they have hitherto remained, & to assume among the powers of the earth the equal & independant station to which the laws of nature & of nature's god entitle them, a decent respect to the opinions of mankind requires that they should declare the causes which impel them to the change.

We hold these truths to be sacred & undeniable; that all men are created equal & independant, that from that equal creation they derive rights inherent & inalienable, among which are the preservation of life, & liberty, & the pursuit of happiness; that to secure these ends, governments are instituted among men, deriving their just powers from the consent of the governed; that whenever any form of government shall become destructive of these ends, it is the right of the people to alter or to abolish it, & to institute new government, laying it's foundation on such principles & organising it's powers in such form, as to them shall seem most likely to effect their safety & happiness. prudence indeed will dictate that governments long established should not be changed for light & transient causes: and accordingly all experience hath shewn that mankind are more disposed to suffer while evils are sufferable, than to right themselves by abolishing the forms to which they are accustomed. but when a long train of abuses & usurpations, begun at a distinguished period, & pursuing invariably the same object, evinces a design to subject them to arbitrary power, it is their right, it is their duty, to throw off such government & to provide new guards for their future security. such has been the patient sufferance of these colonies; & such is now the necessity which constrains them to expunge their former systems of government. the history of his present majesty, is a history of unremitting injuries and usurpations, among which no one fact stands single or solitary to contradict the uniform tenor of the rest, all of which have in direct object the establishment of an absolute tyranny over these states. to prove this, let facts be submitted to a candid world, for the truth of which we pledge a faith yet unsullied by falsehood.

he has refused his assent to laws the most wholesome and necessary for the public good;

he has forbidden his governors to pass laws of immediate & pressing importance, unless suspended in their operation till his assent should be obtained; and when so suspended, he has neglected utterly to attend to them;

he has refused to pass other laws for the accomodation of large districts of people unless those people would relinquish the right of representation, a right inestimable to them, formidable to tyrants alone;

he has dissolved Representative houses repeatedly & continually, for opposing with manly firmness his invasions on the rights of the people;

he has refused for a long space of time to cause others to be elected, whereby the legislative powers, incapable of annihilation, have returned to the people at large for their exercise, the state remaining in the mean time exposed to all the dangers of invasion from without, & convulsions within;

he has endeavored to prevent the population of these states; for that purpose obstructing the laws for naturalization of foreigners; refusing to pass others to encourage their migrations hither; & raising the conditions of new appropriations of lands;

he has suffered the administration of justice totally to cease in some of these colonies, refusing his assent to laws for establishing judiciary powers;

he has made our judges dependant on his will alone, for the tenure of their offices, and amount of their salaries;

he has erected a multitude of new offices by a self-assumed power, & sent hither swarms of officers to harass our people & eat out their substance;

he has kept among us in times of peace standing armies & ships of war;

he has affected to render the military, independant of & superior to the civil power;

he has combined with others to subject us to a jurisdiction foreign to our constitutions and unacknowledged by our laws; giving his assent to their pretended acts of legislation, for quartering large bodies of armed troops among us;

for protecting them by a mock-trial from punishment for any murders they should commit on the inhabitants of these states;

for cutting off our trade with all parts of the world;

for imposing taxes on us without our consent;

for depriving us of the benefits of trial by jury;

for transporting us beyond seas to be tried for pretended offences: for taking away our charters, & altering fundamentally the forms of our governments;

for suspending our own legislatures & declaring themselves invested with power to legislate for us in all cases whatsoever;

he has abdicated government here, withdrawing his governors, & declaring us out of his allegiance & protection;

he has plundered our seas, ravaged our coasts, burnt our towns & destroyed the lives of our people;

he is at this time transporting large armies of foreign mercenaries to compleat the works of death, desolation & tyranny, already begun with circumstances of cruelty & perfidy unworthy the head of a civilized nation;

he has endeavored to bring on the inhabitants of our frontiers the merciless Indian savages, whose known rule of warfare is an undistinguished destruction of all ages, sexes, & conditions of existence;

he has incited treasonable insurrections in our fellow-subjects, with the allurements of forfeiture & confiscation of our property;

he has waged cruel war against human nature itself, violating it's most sacred rights of life & liberty in the persons of a distant people who never offended him, captivating & carrying them into slavery in another hemisphere, or to incur miserable death in their transportation thither. this piratical warfare, the opprobrium of infidel powers, is the warfare of the CHRISTIAN king of Great Britain. determined to keep open a market where MEN should be bought & sold, he has prostituted his negative for suppressing every legislative attempt to prohibit or to restrain this execrable commerce: and that this assemblage of horrors might want no fact of distinguished die, he is now exciting those very people to rise in arms among us, and to purchase that liberty of which he has deprived them, & murdering the people upon whom he also obtruded them; thus paying off former crimes committed against the liberties of one people, with crimes which he urges them to commit against the lives of another.

In every stage of these oppressions we have petitioned for redress in the most humble terms; our repeated petitions have been answered by repeated injury. a prince whose character is thus marked by every act which may define a tyrant, is unfit to be the ruler of a people who mean to be free. future ages will scarce believe that the hardiness of one man, adventured within the short compass of 12 years only, on so many acts of tyranny without a mask, over a people fostered & fixed in principles of liberty.

Nor have we been wanting in attentions to our British brethren. we have warned them from time to time of attempts by their legislature to extend a jurisdiction over these our states. we have reminded them of the circumstances of our emigration & settlement here, no one of which could warrant so strange a pretension: that these were effected at the expence of our own blood & treasure, unassisted by the wealth or the strength of Great Britain: that in constituting indeed our several forms of government, we had adopted one common king, thereby laying a foundation for perpetual league & amity with them: but that submission to their parliament was no part of our constitution, nor ever in idea, if history may be credited: and we appealed to their native justice & magnanimity, as well as to the ties of our common kindred to disavow these usurpations which were likely to interrupt our correspondence & connection. they too have been deaf to the voice of justice & of consanguinity, & when occasions have been given them, by the regular course of their laws, of removing from their councils the disturbers of our harmony, they have by their free election re-established them in power. at this very time too they are permitting their chief magistrate to send over not only soldiers of our common blood, but Scotch & foreign mercenaries to invade & deluge us in blood. these facts have given the last stab to agonizing affection, and manly spirit bids us to renounce for ever these unfeeling brethren. we must endeavor to forget our former love for them, and to hold them as we hold the rest of mankind, enemies in war, in peace friends. we might have been a free & great people together; but a communication of grandeur & of freedom it seems is below their dignity. be it so, since they will have it: the road to glory & happiness is open to us too; we will climb it in a separate state, and acquiesce in the necessity which pronounces our everlasting Adieu!

We therefore the representatives of the United States of America in General Congress assembled do, in the name & by authority of the good people of these states, reject and renounce all allegiance & subjection to the kings of Great Britain & all others who may hereafter claim by, through, or under them; we utterly dissolve & break off all political connection which may have heretofore subsisted between us & the people or parliament of Great Britain; and finally we do assert and declare these a colonies to be free and independant states, and that as free & independant states they shall hereafter have power to levy war, conclude peace, contract alliances, establish commerce, & to do all other acts and things which independent states may of right do. And for the support of this declaration we mutually pledge to each other our lives, our fortunes, & our sacred honour.

The Declaration of Independence

In Congress, July 4, 1776

The unanimous Declaration of the thirteen united States of America,

When in the Course of human events, it becomes necessary for one people to dissolve the political bands which have connected them with another, and to assume among the powers of the earth, the separate and equal station to which the Laws of Nature and of Nature's God entitle them, a decent respect to the opinions of mankind requires that they should declare the causes which impel them to the separation.

We hold these truths to be self-evident, that all men are created equal, that they are endowed by their Creator with certain unalienable Rights, that among these are Life,

Liberty and the pursuit of Happiness.—That to secure these rights, Governments are instituted among Men, deriving their just powers from the consent of the governed, —That whenever any Form of Government becomes destructive of these ends, it is the Right of the People to alter or to abolish it, and to institute new Government, laying its foundation on such principles and organizing its powers in such form, as to them shall seem most likely to effect their Safety and Happiness. Prudence, indeed, will dictate that Governments long established should not be changed for light and transient causes; and accordingly all experience hath shewn, that mankind are more disposed to suffer, while evils are sufferable, than to right themselves by abolishing the forms to which they are accustomed. But when a long train of abuses and usurpations, pursuing invariably the same Object evinces a design to reduce them under absolute Despotism, it is their right, it is their duty, to throw off such Government, and to provide new Guards for their future security.—Such has been the patient sufferance of these Colonies; and such is now the necessity which constrains them to alter their former Systems of Government. The history of the present King of Great Britain is a history of repeated injuries and usurpations, all having in direct object the establishment of an absolute Tyranny over these States. To prove this, let Facts be submitted to a candid world.

He has refused his Assent to Laws, the most wholesome and necessary for the public good.

He has forbidden his Governors to pass Laws of immediate and pressing importance, unless suspended in their operation till his Assent should be obtained; and when so suspended, he has utterly neglected to attend to them.

He has refused to pass other Laws for the accommodation of large districts of people, unless those people would relinquish the right of Representation in the Legislature, a right inestimable to them and formidable to tyrants only.

He has called together legislative bodies at places unusual, uncomfortable, and distant from the depository of their public Records, for the sole purpose of fatiguing them into compliance with his measures.

He has dissolved Representative Houses repeatedly, for opposing with manly firmness his invasions on the rights of the people.

He has refused for a long time, after such dissolutions, to cause others to be elected; whereby the Legislative powers, incapable of Annihilation, have returned to the People at large for their exercise; the State remaining in the mean time exposed to all the dangers of invasion from without, and convulsions within.

He has endeavoured to prevent the population of these States; for that purpose obstructing the Laws for

Naturalization of Foreigners; refusing to pass others to encourage their migrations hither, and raising the conditions of new Appropriations of Lands.

He has obstructed the Administration of Justice, by refusing his Assent to Laws for establishing Judiciary powers.

He has made Judges dependent on his Will alone, for the tenure of their offices, and the amount and payment of their salaries.

He has erected a multitude of New Offices, and sent hither swarms of Officers to harrass our people, and eat out their substance.

He has kept among us, in times of peace, Standing Armies without the Consent of our legislatures.

He has affected to render the Military independent of and superior to the Civil power.

He has combined with others to subject us to a jurisdiction foreign to our constitution, and unacknowledged by our laws; giving his Assent to their Acts of pretended Legislation:

For Quartering large bodies of armed troops among us:

For protecting them, by a mock Trial, from punishment for any Murders which they should commit on the Inhabitants of these States:

For cutting off our Trade with all parts of the world:

For imposing Taxes on us without our Consent:

For depriving us in many cases, of the benefits of Trial by Jury:

For transporting us beyond Seas to be tried for pretended offences:

For abolishing the free System of English Laws in a neighbouring Province, establishing therein an Arbitrary government, and enlarging its Boundaries so as to render it at once an example and fit instrument for introducing the same absolute rule into these Colonies:

For taking away our Charters, abolishing our most valuable Laws, and altering fundamentally the Forms of our Governments:

For suspending our own Legislatures, and declaring themselves invested with power to legislate for us in all cases whatsoever.

He has abdicated Government here, by declaring us out of his Protection and waging War against us.

He has plundered our seas, ravaged our Coasts, burnt our towns, and destroyed the lives of our people.

He is at this time transporting large Armies of foreign Mercenaries to compleat the works of death, desolation and tyranny, already begun with circumstances of Cruelty & perfidy scarcely paralleled in the most barbarous ages, and totally unworthy the Head of a civilized nation.

He has constrained our fellow Citizens taken Captive

on the high Seas to bear Arms against their Country, to become the executioners of their friends and Brethren, or to fall themselves by their Hands.

He has excited domestic insurrections amongst us, and has endeavoured to bring on the inhabitants of our frontiers, the merciless Indian Savages, whose known rule of warfare, is an undistinguished destruction of all ages, sexes and conditions.

In every stage of these Oppressions We have Petitioned for Redress in the most humble terms: Our repeated Petitions have been answered only by repeated injury. A Prince, whose character is thus marked by every act which may define a Tyrant, is unfit to be the ruler of a free people.

Nor have we been wanting in attentions to our British brethren. We have warned them from time to time of attempts by their legislature to extend an unwarrantable jurisdiction over us. We have reminded them of the circumstances of our emigration and settlement here. We have appealed to their native justice and magnanimity, and we have conjured them by the ties of our common kindred to disavow these usurpations, which, would inevitably interrupt our connections and correspondence. They too have been deaf to the voice of justice and of consanguinity. We must, therefore, acquiesce in the necessity, which denounces our

Separation, and hold them, as we hold the rest of mankind, Enemies in War, in Peace Friends.

We, therefore, the Representatives of the united States of America, in General Congress, Assembled, appealing to the Supreme Judge of the world for the rectitude of our intentions, do, in the Name, and by Authority of the good People of these Colonies, solemnly publish and declare, That these United Colonies are, and of Right ought to be Free and Independent States; that they are Absolved from all Allegiance to the British Crown, and that all political connection between them and the State of Great Britain, is and ought to be totally dissolved; and that as Free and Independent States, they have full Power to levy War, conclude Peace, contract Alliances, establish Commerce, and to do all other Acts and Things which Independent States may of right do. And for the support of this Declaration, with a firm reliance on the protection of divine Providence, we mutually pledge to each other our Lives, our Fortunes and our sacred Honor.

About the Author

WALTER ISAACSON has written biographies of Elon Musk, Jennifer Doudna, Leonardo da Vinci, Steve Jobs, Albert Einstein, Henry Kissinger, and Benjamin Franklin. He is also the author of *The Innovators* and the coauthor, with Evan Thomas, of *The Wise Men*. He has been the editor of *Time*, the CEO of CNN, and the CEO of the Aspen Institute. He was awarded the National Humanities Medal in 2023. He is the Leonard Lauder Professor of American History and Values at Tulane and lives with his wife in New Orleans.

A Note on Type

This book is set in Adobe Caslon type, which is known for its elegance, dignity, and legibility. It is based on a typeface created in 1722 by the preeminent London punch-cutter and type-maker William Caslon. Benjamin Franklin imported Caslon's type for his print shop in Philadelphia and chose it for the first printing of the Declaration of Independence.

Also by Walter Isaacson

Available wherever books are sold

or at simonandschuster.com

A Declaration by the Repre

OF AMERICA, in General

When in the course of hu
dissolve the political bands which h

-sume among the powers of the
which the laws of nature & of n
to the opinions of mankind re
which impel them to

We hold these truths to
created equal
inherent & inalien
life, liberty, & the pursuit
-vernments are instituted a
the consent of the governed
becomes destructive of t
or to abolish it, & to institute